Psalm Of The Oppressed

Nkwazi Nkuzi Mhango

Langaa Research & Publishing CIG
Mankon, Bamenda

Publisher:
Langaa RPCIG
Langaa Research & Publishing Common Initiative Group
P.O. Box 902 Mankon
Bamenda
North West Region
Cameroon
Langaagrp@gmail.com
www.langaa-rpcig.net

Distributed in and outside N. America by African Books Collective
orders@africanbookscollective.com
www.africanbookscollective.com

ISBN: 9956-763-52-7

© Nkwazi Nkuzi Mhango 2016

DISCLAIMER
All views expressed in this publication are those of the author and do not
necessarily reflect the views of Langaa RPCIG.

Table of Contents

Foreword

This volume consists of two major books, *The Psalm of the Oppressed* which encourages people to embark on the journey of their true liberation. It uses the song to embolden all oppressed people to go back to their roots and devise methods to liberate themselves–from the yolks of colonialism–be it cultural, political, or economic. Sheep is used as a metaphor. The volume heartens the sheep to move ahead and stop praising alien cultures while abhorring their own. The message is that there is nothing new in new religions, cultures and civilization that Africa didn't have already. That Africa didn't have already.-delete this repetition.

The *Song of Sheep is another book. It* is a satire whose targets are known to the readers and/but it can be construed in any form and all and depends on the understanding of a particular reader.

Essentially, The *Song of the Sheep* can apply to both humans and sheep especially if we borrow from Christianity or colonial connotation of the term. As usual, this type of poetry–apart from attracting readers–is easy to read. And it is oversimplified to make sure that even those who are not experts in poetry grasp something.

Acknowledgements

This piece would not have come to existence without the
assistance of the following
Nesaa My wife Nesaa
Thanks ne ja wana
Thanks for your commitment
Thanks for your support
You always have been there
Whenever there's despair
Writing is not that funny

Our children are also important
They've always been there
Some to cause mayhem
Yet we've to appreciate
Without them
Life would be gloomy
Nthethe, Ndidziwa,
These are our children
Ng'ani Nkwazi Jr and Nkuzi
They've made our home funny

My young brother prof Munyaradzi
You also inspired me brother
Writing has been our buzz
We've no razzmatazz

Let me mention sister Roselyne
What a midwife!
Whenever the book is written
She will give it life
She's always calm and fine
Joanna woods is an icon
When it comes to my works

She edits my rough works
Thanks for a good work Joanna
Langaa is always in the game
Thanks for all

The psalm of the oppressed

The voice was heard
It came from the land
Yes, it came from the land of oppression
The oppressed made a declaration
To stand up and make a proclamation
They're informing all persons
About their new vision

To all who live in this world
Please listen to these powerful words
Sharp words like machetes and swords
They're the words of the doyens
Those who have been oppressed for long

Here comes the book
Yes, the book of books
The book of verses
The verses of all verses
This is your book
Please read this book
This is the book that challenges books
The book that puts others to test
The book brings a great quest
The quest for truth

The book revisits the past
It unveils all deceits
This is the tome of truth
The truth that'll free the mass
This is the tome for the mass
The mass of all that have been ignored
The mass of all who have been oppressed
All those who have been persecuted

This is their book

This is the book for the colonized
It is the book for all whose dreams have never been realized
The book for those whose ways were violated
Yes, it is the tome for the oppressed
All oppressed people
Take your tome

Everybody is invited
Your attention is needed
Attentively please listen
Listen to the nuggets of acumen
This is a declaration
Yes, it is a proclamation
That the oppressed people are making

Open your ears
Receive this good news
It comes from the land and ocean
This news if the foundation
Yes, the foundation for true emancipation
It comes from the ocean of melee
The ocean of skirmishes
Yes, the ocean of rebellions
It is the voice of billions
Yes, billions of the oppressed
Listen to these verses
Hold onto these verses
They're the verses of manumission

The verses are neither new nor old
They're about your creed
The verses have the seal of authenticity
They're based on practicality
They revisit what is regarded as reality
The verses seek to set a precedent

That'll enable all oppressed
To stand up and reason

Take on those who spawned lies
Those who destroyed your ways
As they superimposed theirs
Time for Truth to stand is now
Enough is enough
Nobody should stop this hour
The hour of reckoning
The verses are but a deadline

The verses say it clearly
So hold them dearly
The verses admonish all of you
Never abandon your ways
Never be duped by other ways
Love and keep your ways
Alien ways are not your ways
If others can keep theirs
You, too, have to keep yours
Yours is yours
And theirs are theirs
I'm openly admonishing you
Alien ways are not for you
For those who lost their ways
They'd urgently go back to their roots

Listen to me carefully
Take my words attentively
Nothing is to be done inadvertently
Try to think deeply
You will see the light
I say please stay put
This is a fact
Never be afraid or be cowed
Stand for your right

Restore your dignity

I am but your true vizier
Though it hasn't been easier
To reach at this decision
I've contemplated for long
Now please join the throng
Listen to the words of your awakening
Recite these verses now and then
Pass them to the new generation
For, they're but your weapon
The weapon against cultural colonization
They are the missiles against degradation
They are the surest way out of humiliation
Never bow to any intimidation
Stand for your emancipation

As I was listening
Without pretending
What I sought was but understanding
Why things are this messy
Why are we treated with contempt?
The verses answered this doubt
For, through them I got the meaning
I got the knowledge
Yes, I got the edge
The tool for emancipation
Yes, the emancipation of the oppressed
The restoration of the colonized
This is your premonition

I truly heard the voice
What a powerful voice!
It admonished me not to waive
It urged me to be strong
I stood unmoved like a log
Yet I paid all of my attention

Indeed it was humbling
Yes, it was awakening

Then the power gave me a pen
It told me to make a declaration
The declaration of liberation
For all under colonization
Be it of their brethren
Or that of the foreigners

So, this message is yours
It is hers
It is ours
It is yours

Yes, the message is for all of us
So take it and narrate it
For, the message is but a fact
It is about our plight
The plight of the oppressed

I am the prophet of manumission
For all under the yolk of colonization
Cultural colonization
Economic colonization
All types of colonization
Here comes the prophet
The prophet of reality

Just as it was for other prophets
Many will create some doubts
Especially those who brought their tenets
They'll want me to demonstrate
That what I bring is unique
So, they'll make a critique
Or give me tags
They will call me names

Am I afraid of bad names?
Never, I will stand firm
I will tell them
This is our time
To put things right
I say, so be it
We need our rights back

As I gathered my courage
The voice went on with the message
Then it said loudly
I remember this vividly
As I speak proudly
What the voice confided me intimately
It ordered and encouraged me to preach
It chided me to teach
Here now I come to teach
As I talk about the verses
These verses are yours
They are against theirs
The ones that enslaved us
Yes, take your verses

I firstly was afraid
I felt a little bit timid
I mimicry said at heart
How'll I really tell it?
Then I evoked those who did
Were they believed?
If they did
Why not me?

Others saw the light and fell
What's wrong with me to hear it all?
If others were squeezed and told to say it
Why can't I say it?
The difference however is that

I aim at duping nobody
I aim at fooling nobody
My message is simple
Keep up with your struggle

The voice read my mind
To me it loudly said
"Son don't be afraid"
Then the voice added
"I will give you the powers"
"Son don't be afraid"

As I watched dumbfounded
The voice went on and declared
"Son I know you're astounded"
"Stop your suspicion"
"This is your weapon"
"It'll bring your liberation"

The voice became even louder
It intimidated every ear
It said even more
"Take it and leave here"
"Go to your people and declare"
"Make everything clear"
"What I give is power"
"Take the verses of power"
"They'll liberate the oppressed"

Go tell them the truth
The truth that hurts
This is the truth
It is not lies and myths
Tell your people
Let them keep their struggle
Soon they will be free
If they listen to the verses

These are their verses
Go proudly read the verses
Go teach the verses
These are your verses

The voice gave me these verses
This is how the verses were handed down
The same verses I'm giving you
Receive these verses
They are yours to own
They are the verses of wisdom
They will bring your freedom
They're easy and open verses
They're for all generations
This is your salvation
You who face humiliation
All those who suffer from exploitation
Yes, all those suffering indignation
All those facing intimidation
Go proclaim these verses
Emulate these verses
Recite them in your houses
In your shrines
In your shacks
In your homes
In your sufferings
Never stop reciting the verses

Go sing them
They're your psalm
Declare the cataclysm
To those who dupe you
Stand up and take them on
This is important for you
Never waive or shiver
Stand and declare
Declare the end of the palaver

10

Take these verses
They're totally yours
Tell all people of yours
Tell them the verses are theirs
They must keep them in their hearts
The verses should be kept abreast
These are but their verses

The verses bring your liberty
They're but your light
The light that removes your sufferings
Yes, the verses for new tidings
They, indeed, are the verse of revolution
For those facing exploitation
Hold onto these verses

Your verses are logical ones
They're not sent from dreams
They're not tales or myths
Reliable are the verses
Applicable are the verses
Indeed, they're adorable
They're understandable
Pass them to each other
Recite them time after time
They'll surely deliver you
These are your verses
They're yours completely
They dwell on your emancipation
Yes, for you and your progenies

These verses are the true source
The fountain of the source
They send you to your history
Correct your misrepresented history
Tell your own story

Never let anybody tell your story
Restore your history
This is you glory
Since time immemorial
They stand the test of time
They'll set you free
Emulate these verses
Hold onto these verses

The verses cut like a seesaw
That cuts back and forth
They are constant reminders
They're full of wisdom
They abhor exploitation
They despise sheepishness
They condemn cowardice
They're full of vision
Verses are peaceful
They're not revengeful
Indeed, they seek understanding
They look at the epochs
They revisit ethos

The verses renounce exploiters
Those who eat your flesh
They agitate you to stand
Surely, stand for your rights
These verses are purified
They're well narrated
They're truthful and better
Even though may sound bitter

These verses are aimed at seers
They abhor myopia
Attractive as they are
They're but a disgrace
For the exploiters and haters

They aren't heavy and weighty
They're not easy to ignore
They burn like fire
To pretenders and liars
They're open and clear
To those who hold them dear
They don't mince words
They're for everybody
They aim at your emancipation

The verses have no taboos
Don't keep them in cocoons
Again, watch against goons
Who will come to despise
They condemn fear
Killing the verses means chaos
For those that'll hate them
They state clearly
They order you to take them on
They're not innuendos
Instead, they are your mementos
Everybody will understand them
Make sense of their vision
Take and read as you deem
All those that are suffering

These verses are like a mirror
Yes, they're like a sharpener
For all who are self-conscious
For the lost ones
They'll want to suffocate them
Again, given the verses are weapons
Fight for your emancipation
Regain your freedom
Restore your traditions
Protect your citizens
Use these verses as a weapon

These verses are like embers
They burn ruthlessly
They motivate and rage
They create fear to exploiters
These verses are a big challenge
They're aimed at restoration
Restoration of your civilization
They fight subjugation
Verses are awakening
Take them as a warning
Hold onto your vision
In the end you'll be free
You'll be free and your progenies

These verses will cause vibrations
They'll cause a lot of pulsations
In the hearts of the oppressors
In the mind of hyenas
They'll all face tremors
For the verses will wreak havoc
Many'll end up in shock
As the oppressed start to take stock
The cause of miseries to unlock
The verses will chokehold
Many lies will be unearthed
The truth will be revealed
And the oppressed will know everything

Lo!
I feel sorry for you
Those facing exploitation
I urge you to stand firm
You'll uproot intimidation
You must stand together
As you shy away from division
Whatever you take on

Make sure you're united
Take on those who vend you
Avoid being eaten like fish
Act like fire but not ash

Hear this canticle
I purposely have premeditated
Now I'm leading the way
I aim at all who are exploited
Yes, I know how they're suffering
I've decided to speak openly
I've never stopped agonizing
Looking at how innocent people are suffering
I'm bringing you these verses
Take them for your emancipation

Dear compatriots
Dear patriots
Fear nobody except fear
This is the first law
Never abandon your ways
You'll always be treated like lepers
Nobody should deceive you
Even if you're praised
For abandoning your ways
Never take such rotten prizes
They're nothing but a hoax
Fear them like small pox
Think out of the box
Even if the flummox
You must stand your ground

Fight for equality
Fight for your humanity
I urge young and old
Try the verses you'll see

There are no miracles
Just use your brains
Surely, you'll get your rights

Your mettle will be tested
Your resolve will be tempted
If you don't stay put
You might end up asunder
So, please stay put
Get your act together
Fight harder and harder
You'll get what you want
True emancipation of your people
True rejuvenation of your culture

Without making a U-turn you'll struggle
Without revisiting your past you'll suffer
However life is a struggle
This rule doesn't apply on every angle
Stand for your future
Your future is in your verses
These are the verses
Protect your verses
The way your tormentors protect theirs
Never allow anybody else
To come and abuse your verses again
Make sure you refrain
From being take for a ride

Remember
You're not an island
You're not isolated like Anuta Island
You're not isolated like Easter Island
There are many more like you
Yet, they're different from you
They kept their creeds
You too can copy from them

16

Make sure you keep your creeds

Even the islands of Anuta and Ester stood
They colonized south pacific
They stood
Their power they asserted
The island has a lesson for you
So never panic
Stand united
The verses will emancipate you

I think the message is clear
The language is clear
It is not te taranga paka-Anuta
Or the language spoken in Anuta
So, let us say A Luta
Yes, say A Luta Continua
Means struggle continues
The struggle of your emancipation
The struggle of your perfection
Yes, this is the eon

Beware of your enemies
Those who deceive you
Those who divide you
Warn your children
They'd know their history
Everyone must know his or her adversary
Importantly, make sure you're united
Never be intimidated
Take what's yours
Leave what isn't yours
Guard what's yours
Leave what isn't yours
Your verses know your problems
You need to underscore this
Many'll hunt them

Protect your verses
These are your verses

Recover your names
Take pride in your names
They're but your true identity
Restore your heroes and heroines
Yes, they're Ngwazi and Mthembani
These are your leaders
Glorify your cultures
Promote your mores
Do it together
Dread that is not yours
Respect what is yours
Protect these verses
You'll be safe
Read your verses
The verses have answers
If you use your verses

Praise your valleys and mountains
Go there for pilgrimage
Sing the praise of your plains
Praise your fountains
If others would praise deserts
What's wrong for you to praise your forests?
Sing the glory of your ancestors
Elevate your Gods
Shun all foreign gods
Believe in your Gods

Restore your rituals
Restore your songs
Stop all imitations
You're torturing your hearts
By holding onto what isn't yours
Try to find your origins

You'll dump your troubles
Take it I'm among your seers
Please take your verses

I've opened many alien books
Yes, I've read tons of books
Most of them were carved by crooks
Everything is on tenterhooks
I didn't see any answers
When I see your troubles
It is only through reviving your cultures
That you'll get the answers
Build your societies
As you teach your progenies

I don't want to swear
It will create fear
Whatever that troubles you
You must think independently
With all profundity
For how long will we be dependent?
For how long will we be reticent?
As if we don't have our cultures
Why'd we appropriate?
As if we don't have our own ways
When'll we loan
Especially to those who loan us
Think about this challenge
Read your verses
You'll meet the challenge
Read these verses
They are but your college

To those who are suffering
I see you complaining
Try to find the answers
Please read these verses

19

Instead of reading others'
Read your verses
Go ask your elders
Avoid all fakers
Avoid all pretenders
Take a dip in your past
Open all tomes of the past
Go ask your scholars
You'll get true answers
They're in your verses

Go and study your past
Revisit your history
It is surely perfunctory
Avoid all that's illusionary
Never keep on believing in everything
That the tormentors brought to you
Use your verses to doubt
Never be afraid of anybody
Never be cowed by anybody
Just stay put and focused
Knowing is your right
Knowledge is power
Yes, this power is but emancipation

Never accept intimidation
Never subscribe to being brainwashed
It is only in these verses
You'll self-explore
So, use these verses
You'll answer many questions
You'll stop all doubts
Unveil all lies
Explore these verses
Find your roots
Restore your roots
They're the verses of liberation

These verses burn like fire
They're as precious as sapphire
Ignoring them is but a suicide
Reciting them is but a respite
Recite them without stopping
Proclaim them without any misgiving
In the end,
They'll set you free
For, they're nothing but truth

Read your verses openly
Spread them like bushfire
Love them they'll love you
For, they explain everything to you
Whatever that you need
You've somewhere to explore
Go to your history
Your history is emancipatory
Your history is your trajectory
If you clearly understand the verses
Surely you'll be free

These verses are simple and clear
The verses are short but deeper
Recite them without any fear
Fear nothing but fear
For, fear has turned you into prisoners
With these verses
You've nothing to lose but fetters

Knowledge

Pursue knowledge without stopping
Inquire about everything
Never worry to question everything
Whatever that's wanting
Just treat it suspiciously
Never take things effortlessly
Whatever you think you don't know
Just take it on in order to know
Again, go back to your ways
Compare and contrast everything
Never take things by usage
Make sure no stone is left unturned

You've the right to preach your faiths and feelings
You don't have to fear anybody or anything
This country to you it belongs
You've to make choices
Based on your understandings
Nobody should put you in bonds
Simply because you're expressing your feelings

The verses challenge yes-yes behaviours
The very reasons that brought us sorrows
Believing in things without questioning them
Has brought us bedlam
Look at how you've been exploited
Look at how you've been divided
You now kill one another
A brother hates a brother
If you ask why
It is because of religion
Because of nation
Because of nonsense

Because of illiteracy

Nothing the aliens brought is picture-perfect
However they say theirs are perfect
You know what's and what isn't
Thus, stay put and request
Take on all dogmas
This is your right
Question all hyenas
Question all eaters
Explore their altars
Those who fool you
Those who eat you
Those who dupe you
It is time to put them to rest
It is time to rethink

Let me say something about our knowledge
First of all, I acknowledge our knowledge
My loyalty I pledge
Every society has knowledge
Africa had its own education
Then when aliens came
Condemned our system
They said they found a vacuum
What bunkum!
How could there be vacuum
While Africa was peopled

Fibbers treated our sciences as primordial
They heinously termed theirs contemporary
Their barbarity became exemplary
While ours they brand-named savagery
All was but a mere chicanery
It is sad we believed their lies
We ridiculously went on with this ignorance
Wake up and read the verses

Aliens dubbed their ways *innovative*
Whatever they did was *progressive*
Ours were branded to be primitive
Whatever we did became retrogressive
They regarded us as being naïve
They put themselves above
This mess can't go on
This is why we're to fight on
We're tired of such ruination
Yes, we need to fight on

Tell them your stories of creation
Teach them your civilization
They taught you their ruination
It is now your turn
Preach your civilization
Rejuvenate your lost grandeurs

I know very well
Many people fear tomes
Reading is power
Knowing is power
I know many are busy
Life's become crazy
I know you're confused
You don't know what to follow
So, too, you don't know what to ignore
Also, you know what to explore
You are duped
This has to be stopped
If you dive deep into your past
Discover your glorious past
The message is so simple
By using this principle
You'll know your history
You'll discover your trajectory

To those who were colonized
Do you know the secret behind?
You didn't keep your scripts
They came with their dubious scripts
They outsmarted you
Most even fooled you
As they quoted from their books
Given that you didn't have books
They said you'd to believe
They said you'd not prove
You won't prove whatever you claimed
They held you in bondage
They called their quotes evidence
Even if they were lies and buzzes
What'd you reply
Whenever you're asked
You'd no verses to show
This shouldn't mean you don't know
Now show your verses
These are your verses

Go back to the history
Yes, the history of origins
You'll have many gains
You'll see everything
You'll come to the understanding
That what you thought to be new is old
Question even their gods and God
Please try to investigate
Take nothing for granted
You'll discover the oceans of lies
It is only writings they thought was new
Yet they said everything was new
While it indeed is old
Everything is as old as yours
So, read these verses

You'll make your cases
You'll support your arguments

Didn't Africans have their scripts?
Go deep you'll answer this
Africa had its scripts
They're all over the places
Go to your verses
Explore your pasts
All these will be flawless

They brought their books
They superimposed their creeds
They told their stories
They went ahead
They glorified their stories
They didn't listen to your stories
You're forbidden from telling your stories
Now tell your stories
Make them listen to your sweet stories
The story of glory
The story of the society

You wrongly allowed them to tell your story
They then doctored your story
They abrogated your history
They misconstrued your history
To cap it all
They destroyed your history
Now it is time for you to tell your story
Time for you to rewrite your history

Look at your history
Doesn't it have the story of creation?
Sure, there is a source
The source of creation
There's created a man and woman

Is this really new?
Neither is this a miracle
If anything, it is but a fable
Despite such incongruity
They called their treachery a reality
Their ancestors are your Adam
You must find the name
Find the name of your ancestors
They came with Eve
Try to find your mother
Don't goats know their creation?
What of humans like you?

Every society has ancestors
The difference is the records
You didn't keep your records
Even where you kept your records
You didn't write tomes
Aren't our elders our tomes?
Use them now you'll see
Things have changed
We need to change too
Our elders are dying
We need to start documenting
Whatever they kept about our past
They must be documented
Essentially, this is the essence
The essence of these verses

Others have books
Your elders are your books
You've all reasons
To protect your records
Write your own records
Never let anybody write your history
They'll make everything topsy-turvy
They'll add their lies

They will remove your truth
Restore your ways
Talk about your ways
Read these verses
The verses of your emancipation

Never give up the search
Search and research
Search for your past
Never joke with your past
Your past is your future
Your past is your treasure

If you take my words
As you read these verses
Surely you'll be free
You'll question everything
Everything they brought
You'll seek its authenticity
As you compare with your records
Never glorify what isn't yours
As you abuse what is yours
This is the first slip-up
Wake up
Keep up
Stand up
Speak up
Speak loudly
Do it proudly
Wake and reclaim your past

I see people walking like mad ones
As they glorify what is not theirs
They condemn what is theirs
Get together and search
Protect this speech
Hold on to your values

Protect your verses
You surely will be free
You'll be free from all yolks
You won't be the items for jokes

Why do you act like robots?
Why are you always recipients?
Don't become human cyborgs
They act like dogs
Whatever their masters do
They blindly do
They devour garbage
They glorify babble
Aren't they vagabondage?
You need to be who you truly are
You'll never be what you want to be
You're who you're

Never succumb to any force
Always seek the truth
He who's eyes should see
He who's ears should hear
She who has brains must ponder
It is the right time for us
To revisit our past
So as to reclaim our future

Why'd you be intimidated?
Why being intimidated in your country
Even if you're going to be punished
Whatever that's not yours
Say so that it isn't yours
This is one of your rights
Avoid being duped
You're being exploited
Just like in the era of slavery
I know you suffered a lot

Why can't you wake up now?
Seek your past
The future is in the past

Take your verses
Respect these verses
Stand on my name
I don't speak on my power
I speak on the power of our ancestors
This is my revelation
I bring good news
I say openly
Go back to your roots
This is my will

Mulungu (The Only God)

I've been sent by Mulungu
The one above all gods
This is your true God
The rest are for others
Your God is full of sorrow
Your God says it all
Differentiate Mulungu from aliens

Mulungu is angry
Mulungu wants you to back to your ways
When you abandoned your ways
Everything went astray
Look, everything is now murky
You must go back to your ways
Go back to your true God
The one you knew before new gods
Your God has sent me
Here I am

Here I come
I'm here to pose a problem
Your verses are the solution
They'll free you from shame
They'll free you from suffering

Your God is the power of power
Your God created secretly
Nobody knows his work perfectly
Above all, we were set free
We're not created in pieces
Our faiths are about peace
Not like the alien faiths
The ones that brought violence

I'm talking about the ones
The ones that enslaved us
They abused us
They exploited us
They robbed us
They are still abusing us

Go back to your rituals
Revisit your mores
Go back to your lifestyles
Rejuvenate your names
Live under the only one
Whose name is Mulungu
This is your God
Like Jehovah to Jews
Or Allah to Arabs
Buddha to Indians
Mulungu to Africans

Nobody knows where Mulungu lives
Mulungu doesn't resemble anything
Mulungu doesn't resemble you
God can't resemble feeble creatures like you
Mulungu is above all
Whoever refutes this should come forth
Let him or her show us his or her god
Ours is unseen
All Gods are unseen
This is the truth
Nobody can show his or her God

Our God doesn't require our protection
Mulungu doesn't need our coins
Mulungu is so unique
Mulungu's power is incomparable
Mulungu is the most high
Mulungu's power is for deliverance

Full of forgiveness
Full of rage
Whenever Mulungu decides
Mulungu is neither he nor she
Mulungu is Mulungu
Mulungu punishes betrayers
By turning them into prisoners
Yes, refugees in their own countries

Mulungu is trustworthy
What a trustworthy God!
Does everything justly
Treats all equally
Read these verses
They're the verses of emancipation

These verses are a weapon
Never make any joke
Verses are full of assurance
They're the source of reminder
They're not misleading verses
Just like those alien ones
That came and abused your ways

These verses are but a cure
If you stand by the truth
They'll open your eyes
They'll restore your honour
You'll know the truth
That'll set you free
These verses are reliable
They aim at freeing you
The verses are but a revelation
These verses are like diamonds
Keep and protect them
They are still fierce
They spare no liars

These verses condemn colonizers
Those who want to take you for a ride
They aim at restoring your pride
The verses warn you
Against those who condemn your ways
Those who *eat* others'
As they hide theirs
To such ticks
These verses are poisonous
Don't let them fell these verses
For, the verses are your solutions
Against those confusing you
And all those misleading you

These verses are like a kiln
Like a hell they burn
The verses are but a declaration
They've already been stamped on
They don't need preachers
They don't want astrologers
They're as bitter as gall
For those enslaving you
They'll never like them at all
These verses will cause aliens troubles
For, they unearth their lies
Their times are over
Alien ways must pack and go
We're now going back to our ways
Let's go back to our future
Yes, the future is in the past

The verses are provocative
They shame all who deceive
Their ploy is now over
They won't dupe us any more
They'd not abuse our ways any more

We'd never stomach this
We must take them on
Yes, we'll take on their ways
The same way they did to ours
They must be told to stop
Yes, they'd stop abusing our ways
They've their ways
We've our ways
Everybody with his or her ways
This is justice

These verses are your compass
They'll open your eyes
They are well intended
The verses are shining
Never joke with them
Doing so is your loss
Never entertain it
If they be stolen
Those used to doing so
Those used to steal whatever is yours
These verses are a sign
The sign of your emancipation
Read these verses through thick and thin

These verses are like an arrow
Pigs won't like them
Read them without budging
Read them without dreading
Those that hate them
Tell all those apes
To stop monkey business
Abusing our ways
Condemning our ways
Time for telling them is now

Let's pay them back

These verses are education
They're very important
Knowledge they inculcate
They're full of wisdom
They inculcate discipline
Follow all rules
Follow all mores
That your ancestors handed down
Put more efforts
To reclaim your lost past
You must know your enemies
These who poisoned your ways
So as to force you abandoning them
Now it is your time
Yes, it is time
Time to go back to your noble roots

The verses condemn *holier than thou*
That the alien played on you
Nobody should be you master
You're your own masters
Nobody should make you servants
You're a civilized people
You've never eaten each other
Or enslaved one another
You've never colonized others
Don't allow others to keep colonizing you
Those who want to keep on dividing you
Please tell them openly no
Tell them to pack and go
Let them take their ego

I'm talking to vagrants
Those that treated you like refugees in your countries
These verses are yours

Take them and read
They'll show you the way home
I know you need to go back home
Home where you belong
Never stop to throng
Where you're respected
Home where you're protected
Your home is where you get your rights
So, your origin doesn't matter
What matters is how you're treated

Never stop asking
Do it without pleading
The question should be
Where is home?
The one you know as home
Please go home
If somebody's taken your home
Tell him or her to go home
Tell them to all feel at home
By equally living in this home
Again, where is home?
Is home where I was born
If so, am I respected and protected
What of foreigners that are protected
While I am not
Let's make home our home for all
Stop discrimination
Stop exploitation
Stop colonialism
Then we'll all be at home
Respect each other's ways
Let's make home true home for all

Don't say you're not warned
Never say that you're not told
You're earnestly told

Save that you ignored
Now that we repeat
We tell you the same fact
Truth is in this text
Grab it and use it

Hyenas

There came hyenas in sheep's clothing
They turned things upside down
They damaged everything
They preached the gospel of destruction
They put our ways asunder
They came with their concoctions
They robbed us what is dear to us
Now that we've seen everything
For long we suffered from everything
Wake up my friends
Take these words
Yes, take these verses
They'll set you free
They'll reclaim your lost glee

Impostors said our ways are evil
Shamelessly as if theirs weren't evil
Theirs is the work of the devil
By all means they're evil
Time to dispel their myths is now
Let's seriously do it right now
Let's tell these ungodly people
That ungodly is their gospel

Never be duped by sweet promises
Yes, you're promised paradises
This is, indeed, ridiculous
Didn't they find you in your paradise?
If not, why did they come?
Our paradise is real and big
It is full of everything
Haven't you lived in the paradise?
Sadly, when they promised you their *paradise*

You offered your true one
For the promise of illusionary one!

Tell them their legacy
Remind them of their fallacy
Jog them through colonialism
Remind them of their nihilism
Yes, remind them of their vampirism
Retell them of slavery
Some still think we're still slaves
Don't they call us abid?
To mean we are slaves
To them we're but infidels
However one strives
To them we'll never cease to be slaves
Is it wrong to call them slaves of their malice?

Ask all those slave masters
Didn't they rape our sisters?
Didn't they castrate our brothers?
Why becoming brethren now
Why not then but now?
Why not then they sold us
Can true brethren sell others?
Can true sistren vend others?
What brotherhood is this?
Can true brothers call others bad names?

Calling us their brothers is hypocrisy
Why calling us brothers after violating us?
They must first redress us
They call us their brothers
If they're our true brothers
They'd not have robbed us
They'd not have enslaved us
They'd not have colonized us
This is really ridiculous

They've no brethren in us
We're who we're
They're who they're
This the only truth
The rest is but a myth

Colonialists committed gross inhumanity against us
Yet, they later called us their brothers
Are we real their brothers and sisters
Who's fooling whom hither?
This is the story we need to remind them
I know they pretend to have forgotten their crimes
Let's keep on reminding them
To show them we know them
We still remember their criminality
They'd not dupe us with equality
Why now not then

Fear not their bad names
They're but tools of intimidation
Never be cowed
Just stay put and alert
They want to instill fear in you
Let them call you pagans
They call you infidels
They call you kaffirs
Who are they to you?
Aren't they the same?
This is tit for tat
You call me that
I call you the same

If they call you names
Reciprocate by calling them names
Never feel any shame
Take them on
Feed them with the same dynamism

41

Give them the same anathema they brought
Yes, treat them exactly the same
Don't succumb before their scam
Glorify your names
Apply your mores
Never import names
What a shame!

Remember what's in names?
They brought their ridiculous names
What meaningless names!
What stupid surnames of theirs
They felled ours
Ask them to take our names
They'll think you've mental sickness
Yet they called us all sorts of names
Isn't this mental sickness
Why calling us
Gibbons
Stones
Abids
Cats
Swords
And whatnot

Let me warn you again
Yours was condemned
Simply because yours was not documented
You kept no written records
Again, they defied science
As they laughed at your undocumented
Ask them to prove their claims scientifically
You'll hear them complaining sarcastically
Better with Fibonacci sequence
Better with Platonic solids
They've some resonance
When it comes to cultural nonsense

I see no evidence

Didn't Africans teach Fibonacci?
Yes, the Africans so-called moors did
Moors taught Fibonacci indeed
They taught him the science of numbers
Sadly, they didn't keep records
Some say they kept records
That ended up being destroyed
Despite such truth
Colonizers say Africa didn't have science
Who discovered fire?
Who erected Egyptian Pyramids?
Aren't pyramids miracles by themselves?
Aren't they a very advanced science?
Didn't we conserve our ecology?
Whoever that denies you such knowledge
Should go and study African etiology
If such a person fails to appreciate our technology
He or she can go study garbology
Even there they'll get knowledge

Tell those who claim to perform miracles
Their miracles are inconceivable
Their claims are deplorable
They call lies miracles
And they call reality lies
Didn't we've real miracles?
Aren't they all over the place?

Go to many parts of Africa
Every place has its wonders
Human prints on stones
Aren't there in South Africa?
You'll see hanging objects
Aren't there such wonders?
Go to stone houses of Zimbabwe

Remember golden stools of Asante
Aren't these miracles?
Aren't they science?

Figure 1 Asante's golden stools

Some said Africa didn't have technology
What fallacy!
Didn't we teach them how to smelt iron?
Didn't we teach them irrigation?
They forgot one fact
Africa is a cradle of mankind
If Africa is the cradle of mankind
So, too her God is the God of Gods

Evidences are everywhere
Go to the south Pacific
Didn't Africans conquer Pacific?
Isn't this scientific?
However the weather is horrific
Africans colonized south Pacific
Before the coming of Europeans
Such act was treated as magic

It gave Europeans a shock

Go to Easter Island
See those magnificent statuettes
Aren't they a miracle?
Go even deeper
Look at how Anutans fish
They fish without any gear
They breathe under water
They carry no breathing devices
They perfected this science
Nobody's ever beat such a science
They succeeded after felling our science

Liars despise our ways
They destroyed our sciences
They robbed us of our skills
They superimposed their evil ways
They called ours backward ones
They call theirs progressive ones
Are they really progressive?
Was slavery progressive?
Was colonialism progressive?
Is imperialism progressive?
Why don't they agree theirs is oppressive?
Their ways are abusive
They destroyed ours

They went on saying theirs is new
Phew!
Is there anything new under the Sun?
They say ours were unwritten
It is true ours was not written
Again, wasn't ours unspoken?
Our philosophy was crammed
Despite being unwritten
Impostors branded theirs advanced

45

Just because theirs are written
When you ask about them being proven
They start calling your names

Why writing something that's kept at hearts?
Weren't our stories well-kept?
Go ask our griots
Go interrogate our seniors
Weren't they books?
Weren't they CDs at the time?
Will the coming generation laugh at us
They'll store things differently
Won't they use gadgets to store what we write?

Every epoch has its technology
Every epoch has its knowledge
Nothing is better than another
If it is measured according its period
Everything is living
It grows from one stage to another
Everything is progressing
Nothing is stationary

When colonialists came and duped us
They proclaimed to have conquered us
All are but mere lies
There's nothing like conquering us
Why don't they talk about unique generosity?
Didn't they abuse our generosity?
Yet, they dubiously called it gullibility
Was it really naivety?
Let's be serious
As we avoid such ignorance
They called their ignorance knowledge
They called our knowledge nonsense
Again, in the real sense
Knowledge is knowledge

All knowledge were created
So, too all knowledges can be advanced

When colonialists arrived
Africans grossly erred
They thought they're civilized
They treated them kindly
The hosts thought they'd have reciprocated
Instead, they took us for a ride
They betrayed our trust

Pretenders as they've always been
Came in sheep's clothing
Like lambs, we let them in
Thinking they're our akin
We just ended up being eaten!
Can you call this civilization?

Like hyenas,
They devoured us
Like serpents,
They poisoned us
They pitied one against another
We ended up drawn wide asunder
Like warthogs,
They spoiled our water
With all sorts of feces
They disgraced our mores
Had we known they're unthankful
Surely we'd have been watchful
All the same we erred
Here we're in melancholy

Colonizers condemned everything we owned
It is only our foods and minerals
That they didn't judge

They called us savages
They called us uncivilized
Were we truly uncivilized!
Aw!
What insults!
Were we cowards?
What a disgrace!

How'd we be uncivilized with all such generosity?
How'd we be with all such humanity?
Our tormentors forgot everything
Our generosity became nothing
How do you call such a gambit?

They ruined our reputation
They created excoriation
They heaped insults on us
An insult after another
Colonialists didn't bother
They brought their violence
They destroyed our peace
Here we're now in distress!

Those who don't know us
Erroneously think it's out of cowardice
That we ended up in such quandaries
No, the crystal clear truth is
We're betrayed by our kindness
Our generosity brought us miseries

Figure 2 Giant statues in Ester Island

Figure 3 Ancient stone sites in Zimbabwe

Song of the sheep

Baa baa baa is the sound of the sheep
Many are used to this sound of the sheep
Here I bring the song of the sheep
Yet, this song is a unique song of the sheep
The sheep in this song isn't singing
Instead, the sheep is wailing
It is crooning a song of sorrow
The sheep is wailing for tomorrow
It is the song of its sorrow and miseries
In this song, the sheep does weep
This is the song of the sheep
Yes, the song of all sheep
Wherever they may be
This song is theirs indeed
We now call upon all sheep
Please come all sheep
This jingle is yours

Instead of singing "baa, baa" we're used to
The sheep's singing "no, no" we're not used to
The sheep are saying enough is enough
It sings about justice
It condemns injustices
This is but a changed sheep
The sheep that wants other sheep to change
Let's sing with the sheep
Let's sing "no, no, no"
Let's join sheep to say "no"
Let's join them to say enough is enough
Let no one blow off
To inflict more biff

All sheep need to come and sing this song

This song is for all sheep
Black
White
Yellow
Coloured
You name it
Come all sheep
Come join others
Sing this song of yours

Come my brothers and sisters
Come join me in this quest
Come all sufferers
You *sheep* that need help
Yes, come every sheep
In whatever barn you are in
Come join
Come listen
Come learn
Come croon
This is your tune

I'm an innocent sheep
I'm a harmless sheep
The difference is I'm a seer sheep
That wants to admonish all sheep
Beware of the trap
Yes, there's a trap
I can see it clearly

Listen to my wisdom
Here I proclaim
As innocent as a lamb
Yes, I'm the lamb
The lamb with aplomb
I'm sure we'll triumph

I'm a sheep facing vicious hyenas
Not one or two hyenas
I'm facing tons and tons of hyenas
I see hyenas everywhere
Liberation is nowhere
Except to declare war
I am declaring war against hyenas
I call upon all sufferers
Come join me in this war
It is but your war
The war for your recovery

I see hyenas
Yes I can see hyenas
They're all over the place
The entire place is messy
Hyenas have no mercy
They're ruthless
They stop on nothing but our demise

These hyenas used to be among us
We know they're beasts
We thought they're our kind
Just before we reckoned
We're all under the plague

Do you remember this?
Try to recall
Remember the time
When we faced lions
Weren't they today's hyenas?
Weren't they with us?
Again, when lions left
They took over the clout
They turned us into their beasts of prey
They started killing us
Since then they've been killing us

Honorable hyenas

I can see hyenas in their expensive vehicles
Some are in classy suits
Some are trinkets
I see them in their castles
I see them eating flesh
Their lives are posh
They don't eat grasses like us
I see them on top of us
They're devouring us
I see hyenas
Honorable hyenas

You hyenas
Yes, I'm talking to you
Yes, you hyenas
Powerful hyenas
The high and mighty of hyenas
Hyenas
Hyenas
You came from the forest
Always you've eaten us
You've invited other beasts
You're now feasting on us
We need to stop this cruelty

Where's your home?
Why abandoning the forest
Why invading our city
Aw!
Wow!
I wonder!
How do you laugh at me?
Well, the sage told me

Ape doesn't see its bottoms?
Have you ever seen your bottoms?
How can you see your bottoms?
While you don't look back

Hyenas robbed us of our freedom
They turned our barn into a fiefdom
They created a doom
Here we're in the doom
Aren't we doomed?
Aren't we butchered?
Aren't we used and abused
Who are we?
We're innocent sheep
You're an innocent sheep
She's an innocent sheep
They're innocent sheep

I'm talking of honorable hyenas
Yes, untouchable hyenas
Sacred hyenas
You ferocious and corrupt hyenas
Hyenas with all muscles
The powers you pass on to your progenies
These are the hyenas I'm talking about
You know what I'm talking about
You know whom all this is all about
Yes, I'm talking to you
I'm talking about you
And it is only you
That I'm fighting

This note is for mighty hyenas
Yes, this speech is for the hyenas
I've no apology
So, too, I've no eulogy
Mine is but philosophy

Aimed at awakening the sheep
Take this mantra dear sheep
Make use of it
Indeed, it is but your feat

Yes, I'm talking of hyenas
The ones that cling to the top
They want all their relatives to be on top
Theirs is always clinging to the top
Power is their top priority
Even if it means to destroy humanity
Power and hyenas
Are but inseparable

Blind hyenas

Honorable hyenas are blind
They're the creatures of their own kind
They want to eat all sheep
They are careless about tomorrow
Why don't they understand?
If they decimate the sheep
What'll they eat tomorrow?

Yes, I'm talking to you blind hyenas
You who have never seen tomorrow
I can see you everywhere
The situation is peculiar
I see you enjoying everything
Yes, you're in control of everything
I can see he hyenas
I can see even she hyenas
What I see are hyenas
Yes, the congregation of hyenas
That's what makes my future grim

See?
Hyenas have occupied everything
Whatever that's meaningful
Is in the dirty hands of the hyenas
Whatever that's beautiful
It is owned by hyenas
Sheep have but nothing
Sheep are but the oppressed
Sheep are endangered
Soon sheep will become extinct

I see all sorts of hyenas
Fat hyenas

Old hyenas
Young hyenas
They all share one thing
They're gluttonous
They're ridiculous
They are all eyeless

I see hyenas amongst us
They're conspiring to devour us
They've always devoured my kin
They feed on me
They live on me
Yes, it is me
Yes, me who makes such hyenas fat

Fat hyenas
All hyenas you see everywhere
They all feed on me
They feed on you
They feed on him
They feed on her
Yes, if you're a sheep
They'll always devour you
It is solely upon you
To stand and take them on

Sometimes, hyenas pretend to be kind
They always pretend
That they love the herd
Never subscribe to this ruse
It is but your demise

Hyenas dupe sheep that they're the same
They preach the equality of *beasts*
My colleagues take it from me
Hyenas will never be the same as sheep
If anything

57

Hyenas are but the killers of sheep

Let me tell you something
When hyenas preach equality
Mind you
They dupe you
Never believe anything
For, eating you is the in-thing
Yours is but vulnerability
Hyenas' words have no credibility
They're but bankrupt and empty
They end up becoming humpty-dumpty

Listen to your sage
This is my message
Sheep need unity
By all means form sorority
Then stand up and fight
Never buy into hyenas' gambit
My friends you'll regret
For, theirs is only carnage
So, always be cagey
Every hyena is bogey
Be it old or young
Better send hyenas to the cage
That's when you'll rummage

Brazen *hyenas*

Hyenas
Blatant hyenas
You came from the forest
You joined us
You sang the same song with us
You ate grasses with us
You duped us
You spoke of liberation of beasts
You preached the gospel of better politics
The politics of equality
The politics of mortality
The politics of development
We sheep wrongly thought you'd change
Our hope was change
Yes, you brought change
The difference is in this change
You turned peace into carnage
You committed the sacrilege
Like any politician you duped us
We wrongly thought
That you hyenas have seen the light
We thought you'd stop the carnage
Now we are in bondage
You've invited other hyenas
You're feasting on us
Then you still laugh at us
You think we are crazy
For not confronting you

You took our freedom
You took our kingdom
Yes, you took the kingdom of the barn
You dubiously turned it into a den

You hoodwinked us
You seduced us with democracy
You promised us better life
You promised us worthy life
You promised us posh life
Had we known
You meant your posh life
Had we known
We're playing with a knife

Dear unscrupulous hyenas
We didn't know it was but conspiracy
Here now we're in anarchy
Yes, we're under hyena's mobocracy
You've played one against another
Here we're stuck and doomed
We're confused
Who'll help us?
Who'll understand us?
Remember guys
We're but innocent sheep

This barn isn't your home
Why abandoning the forest
Why invading our home
Yes, the barn is our home
All beauties you enjoy are ours
You feed on us
Like ticks, you exploit us
Like hemi-parasitic plants
You depend on us
Do we depend on you?
How can we depend on you?
What do you have to depend on?
What parasites!

Hyenas,

You preached justice
You preached coexistence
Everything you preached was nice
What happened in the end?
Here we're manacled
Sheep are devoured
Hyenas
Despite all this
You still laugh at us!
How dare you
Do you think this will go on?
Hear all hyenas
Sheep are awake now
We are ready to take you on
We want to expel you
Yes, we'll expel you from our state houses
We'll kick you out of our offices
We sheep are now declaring
The land of sheep must be free
Sheep must rule themselves
Yes, this time is for sheep
Yes, only sheep

Aw!
Wow!
I wonder
How do you laugh at me?
Well the sage told me
Ape doesn't see its rump
Have you ever seen your rump?
How can you see it?
While you don't look back
Do you pay any hoot?
Can camel see its hump?

I'm still wondering
I can't believe

When I remember
The humble persona you're
When you brought your democracy
Yes, you brought parity
That ended up being our expiry
You espoused impartiality
You practiced injury
What quacks!
What fibbers!

We didn't know it was a hoax
We can now see its crux
Yes, we see the apex
Everything is but tex mex
Ours is but nix
When we remember this hoax
That you gave good names
We indeed feel worse
Again, there's no remorse
Ours is to seek recompense
By evicting all hyenas
We need them behind bars
Ours is to take this course
The course of educating all sheep
O sheep, wherever you are, wake up
Stand up
Gang up
Speak up
Let's fight for our rights

Look now we're dying
We're being tortured
We've nowhere to lean on
We've nowhere to go to
Nobody understands us
Our masters have abandoned us
Yes, we need somebody to turn to

We need a place to go to
We invite every person
We need to take on these hyenas
Yes, the hyenas that are feasting on us
We're now endangered
Indeed, we're threatened
The threats are unimaginable
Threats
Threats
Hyenas are threatening us

These hyenas conned us
They mingled with us
Yet, in the end; they tamed us
They said we're all beasts
Look at how they maltreat us
All beasts aren't equal
Are they truly equal?
How if some are glorified
While other are fried

The hyenas living extravagantly aren't like sheep
The sheep they exploit
The sheep that pick up the tab
The sheep that are refugees in their barn
The sheep whose barn was turned into a den
Call it a den hunk
Everything is thunk
We're under politics of junk
However our Lord we thank
Sheep are awake
We're ready to talk
We're ready to fight
Yes, we're awake
Please everybody awake

Though we eat grasses

Where are the grasses for us to eat?
They're all dry
Do we've anything to mislay
Why shouldn't we strike a match?
After all grasses are dry
Do we've anything to fail?
Sheep have all reasons to fight
Let's die fighting
Rather than living watching
All sheep must hearken
The battle they must join
We're sure we'll win
Our unity is our win

We're in big troubles
Who'll help us out of these troubles?
Please come and help us
Why all this?
Masters why?
Why are we facing all this?
How did we lose our home?
Masters, help us to force hyenas to go home
Please masters; let's send them to their home
All hyenas must go back to their home
We plead with you good masters
Let's give it stab fellas
Let's take on hyenas
They must be confined to their true home
The wilderness is their home

Master, here we're tired,
We decline,
Let's force hyenas to hunker down
Here we can't understand
Here we're under hyenas' orders
Master, help us,
Master, listen to us

64

Don't ignore us
The world must hear us
Never keep quiet

Please masters
Help us,
Stop supporting these hyenas
Why can't you support us?
Don't you know you feed on us?
Just like hyenas do
You still will feed on us
You'll drink our milk
You'll use our manure
You'll eat our products

Let's send hyenas back to where they belong
Demote them to where they belong
Let's move them right away
Hyenas should go back to their ways
Yes, to the wilderness where they naturally belong
They must go
When are they to go?
We need to know
Just right now

Masters, just tell us
When are we seeing them off?
We're tired of their threats and scuffles
They're fighting over us
They're treating us badly
Are we supposed to be treated like this?
Are beasts supposed to treat others like this?
Are we supposed to let hyenas usurp our powers?
If they stay it means this is not home
If this is their home
Where is our home?
If this is true

65

Then tell us the truth
Where is home
Tell us we'll vanish
We'll run like a horse
So that we can go there
Where we're going to be protected
Where hyenas won't reach us
Where hyenas won't feast on us
Yes, home where we belong

Our home isn't a hyena's den
We want them to go to their den
Master we swear
We ask you to send hyenas to the wilderness
We wish they'd soon evaporate
Hyenas must disappear from here

Everybody's the right to belong
Sheep belong to the barn
Hyenas be they docile still belong to the den
Let's respect nature's proclamation
Thus everybody must belong
Yes, everybody must belong
To where he/she naturally belongs

Then the master replies
As he laughs
"I can hear your cries"
"I know your pains"
"Yet I can help in this"
"Sheep use your brains"
"Do you think I am to help?"
"Why can't you help yourselves?"
"Why not form a front?"
"Why can't you confront them?"
"I have a lot to do"
"I am sorry my friends"

To all beasts

Figure 4 a barn

The master adds
"Hyenas are beasts"
"By the way"
"When will you face these fiends?"
"Yes, I am the master"
"I get whatever I want"
"What have I with your feuds?"

The sheep replies
"Please master understand me"
"I plead and beseech you"
"Master understand me"
"Please help me"
"Take your hyenas away"
"Do so right away"
"We're tired of their carnage"
"We're fed up with their hunger"
"We're feed up with their bigotry"

"Master, I provide you with proteins"

"I've always taken your instructions"
"Never shall I ignored your orders"
"I've always been faithful"
"Why are you allowing such tortures?"
"Is this the way you appreciate my humbleness"

Some hid my products in your home
They wanted to use them in the future
They end up losing the whole kit and caboodle
You enjoy the loot
They just die broken hearted
Didn't they know that hyenas will be caged?
Didn't they know that their pomp is but temporal one?
Now that everything is clear
Still other hyenas have some products to stash!

Wait, the master will chip in
Hey, sheep, are you mad or what
Do you think they'd eat your products?
Whatever they bring is mine
Do you remember that a hyena from the forests of DRC?
He killed many sheep and stashed fresh in my freezers
Remember the one from the forests of Nigeria that did the
same
Do you need more?
The hyena in Libya once brought camel meat
All hyenas above stashed their loot
None of them ate it
They didn't know I am a hyena
Yes, I am a hyena like them
I cheated them
Don't cheat yourself
Never rely on me
We are all the same

Everybody knows
We created all these zoos

68

We established all those barns
We saw the future
We know they would fight one another
We put them asunder
We divided you
We wanted to keep our grip on you
It is upon you
Get your acts together
There is no godfather

Master I now understand
These hyenas are losers
They're insane and crazed
Kick them out of the powers
Sheep want to rule themselves
Sheep should be ruled by sheep
The sheep of this kind don't need a Shepherd
It becomes even worse when a hyena becomes a shepherd
We sheep are tired of hyenas
We want all hyenas out of our home
If the barn we share is hyenas' home
Then sheep must go home
Where is our home?
If the barn is ours
Then hyenas must go home

The sheep need to go
Otherwise hyenas have to go
The sheep are ready to go
On foot we'll go
By borrowing we'll go
Without riding on the horse
Still we'll go
Slowly we'll go
In a hurry I'll go
We're tired of living in the barn
Yes, where there's no justice

Where everything is corrupt and messy
We better know one thing
If this is our home
Then hyenas should be sent parking
They've nothing here

Theirs has always been destruction
They invented corruption
They embarked on our destruction
Greed is their slogan
Selfishness has always been their weapon
Sheep have lost everything here
It is only laws to which to adhere
Otherwise, they've lost everything
They've lost their wellbeing
Hyenas have squandered everything
Despite eating everything
They eat with both hands
They even don't wash their hands
They'll never get satisfied
Hyenas are hyenas indeed
Even if they're honorable hyenas
Hyenas are hyenas
Even if they get power
Hyenas are naturally evil
Under them we're vulnerable

Sheep need their home
Why shouldn't they have a home?
Everybody deserves a home
Yes, the place to call home
Even wondering birds have homes
Whenever they fly and hunt around
In the end they go back to their abodes
They come home with pride

Birds' nests are their homes

70

However rudimentary they might be understood
Birds are always proud
Sheep need hyenas to go home
Please hyenas go home
Don't wait to be forced
Your time to go is now
Sheep's barn can't be a den
A den is a den
And a barn is a barn

Hyenas will never be good to sheep
Hyenas will never love sheep
Sheep and hyenas must not mingle
Sheep need to rid their barn of hyenas
Yes, we sheep are tired of hyenas
We need to purge them just now
This is my wisdom
Hyenas have no decorum
They deserve no concern
Let them go to hell
There's where they fit well

Look at me
I've lost everything here
I see nothing to own
All I know is derision
Surely this is not home
I say this is not home
I want to go home
I didn't fall from a tree
I must have a home
Even trees have home
Wondering birds have home
Why not me?

Why turning a barn into a den
Sheep are not hyenas

Hyenas' home is a den
Sheep's home is a barn
The two are distant and different
They've different etiquette
Why'd they be mixed?
Why hyenas should be vindicated
As sheep are vexed
We're tired of this anomaly
Please, hyenas go to the boonies

We sheep say it loudly
We declare it boldly
The barn is our home
The den is hyenas' home
Our barn is our state houses
Hyenas have no state houses
There is bad odor
They've defecated on our state houses
All hyenas are on the loose
They're devouring us
They've invited all *bêtes noirs*
They're comfortably enjoying the spoils
They're stashing the loots
Far, far away from the barn

Ours always are hays
Theirs are always sirloins
Hyenas should live on bones
Our hyenas live on steaks
Hyenas should live in feces
Ours live in posh mansions
You can't reconcile such creatures
However, there is one way for peace
Send hyenas to the wilderness
Stamp them out of our barn
Let them go to their den

With hyenas on the wheels
We're left with no choice
It is only to tell them this truth
Hyenas go to the wilderness
With you we're hopeless
You've defecated on our bliss
Ours is only compunction
Yours is destruction
We've been turned into homeless
We've nothing

Ours is worrying
We're vended in the marketplace
Then we're told we're at home
What type is this home?
What a deceptive home!
Hyenas go home
It is time for you to go
Go hyenas go

Go hyenas go wicked creatures
Go without turning thy heads back ever
The game is up and over
Go creatures of hell, cowards in your own light
Go hyenas go down standing like a dolt
In flames go down like that
In a shame go even faster
Go honorable hyenas go
Go, other hyenas will go
They soon will follow
Go leave the mark back
Go like goons and stooges
Go the ignoble way go.

Go the barn will remember you
Just as a symbol of megalomania
Go hyenas go

Go hyenas go
It is time for you to go
Never look back, go
Go *bêtes noirs* go
It is time for you to go.

Go to your no-go
Go
Go
It's time for hyenas to go
Go, go, and go
Don't turn back, go!
Those that you used to butcher
Are now coming in scores
Cornered you are now
Go hyenas go

Injustices

However I live in a no-go
Yet wherever I go in my no-go
I just see injustices above all
All of my life I've danced this puerile fandango
I see a lot of greed
I've seen hyenas' corrupt creed
Like weeds they've spread
They've me on whom to feed
From my flesh and down to bone
Those I thought were with me
They've long abandoned me
They're feasting on me
Those I wrongly thought we're the same
They turned against me
What do you expect when you're ruled by hyenas?
No sheep will be safer before hyenas
They're feasting on us
What injustices!

It pains beyond bearing
Hard is imagining
How can we make do with such a thing?
It is always hard to twig
It becomes even trickier
To understand how powerful hyenas are
There are a lot of hyenas with immense power
We're under the control of such hyenas
We are under powerful but stupid hyenas
Those who defecate in the holy of the holy
Those who are rotten morally
Bêtes noirs and silly

It is easy to know the hyenas
Look around
They're all over the place
They've held their ground
They've tighten their grip on us
They feed on us
They used to be ones among us
When they betrayed us
They created their own class
The class of hyenas
These hyenas are unique
Never confuse them with the one you know
These types of hyenas are sick
I know you know
You know what I mean

Hyenas have destroyed our lifestyle
They pushed us in shacks
Their life is comfy
Ours is messy
To us they've no mercy
They chew our flesh
What injustice!

They sent us into the byres
They live in the granges
Hyenas underwent changes
They now enjoy powers
They've wrongly became noble ones
Everything is in their hands
They even own us
They've taken over from us
Now they're doing their injustices
With impunity they rule us
With cruelty they oversee us
Try to think deeply
Don't you see them really?

Don't we know them clearly?
Don't they know themselves truly?

Hyenas are always vampires
Even if they rule empires
They deserve to end up in fires
This is the way we can contain their greed
They need to live behind bars
This how we can contain their evil deeds
Hyenas are always guilty
They're guilty of their criminality
Sheep should never seek conviviality
Conviviality with hyenas is but death

However they turned us into sheep
Before we were not sheep
When on us they tightened their grip
We officially became sheep
But if you look at us deeply
All animals are equal
The difference however is
They're hyenas
We're sheep
Yes, we are innocent sheep
They're guilty hyenas

Wrongly one might think we're the same
Simply because we all have skins
Sheep and hyenas will never be the same
Even if we're all beasts
Hyenas are cursed beasts
We sheep are innocent beasts
There can't be any reconciliation
Hyenas deserve to live in the prison

To nicely exploit us
Hyenas put us in squeezed shacks

We live in queues
We live in chaos
Our lives have become meaningless
What we know is only mess
They live in showiness
Hyenas have become our masters

They eat what they want
We eat what we get
Our lives are totally different
Theirs is opulent
Ours is unfortunate
Yet they say this barn is ours
While in practicality it is theirs
They made our barn theirs

Do they think we'll make their den ours?
Who wants to live in a den?
Isn't the barn better than the den?
This is why they abandoned their dens
To end up colonizing our barns
In the end however
We are all beasts
We all look on our master
The one with real power
Yes, the master
The master of abracadabra
Yes, the master of chicanery

Hyenas are brutal
Whatever they do is illegal
They care little about sheep
These creatures are creepy
Their deeds are spooky
What betrayals!
What jackals!
However they're animals

78

Yes, hyenas are beasts like us
Again, when they got power
We ceased to be equal beasts
Yes, when the master handed them power
Our bond was broken
They became our monsters
They used to be our akin
They filled in the place of the masters
Differently from the masters
They are still beasts
What they know is only bestiality
They destroyed our charity
They're hyenas in sheep's attire
Let me make this clear
Hyenas used to be treated like beasts
We, too, used to be exploited like beasts
We're sheep
And they're hyenas

I've never stopped wondering
It pains upon hearing
Can you believe such con?
Hyenas dictate our destiny
They've taken our barn
What else should they do?
Aren't we on the Carrefour?
Haven't they have us to devour
Who cares when sheep fall?
Who listen when sheep yell?
What a conspiracy!
What fraudulence!

We live in shacks
There's nothing left for us
We suffer and nobody cares
No medical services

79

Nothing but deaths
When we complain
They just rejoin
"Those are sheep"
They add
"Theirs is knife"
Others say
"They're suffering because of their sheepishness"
What!
Do you hear that?
Yes, we need to fight
We need to fight sheepishness
We need to fight all hyenas

When we recall the hindmost
The time when we fought for sovereignty
We only feel pains
We end up in qualms
We curse our trust in them
The day we trusted them
We created our own mayhem

Mulungu!
Who thought things would become messy
Who'd envision such a mess?
Who'd expect such injustices?
Here we're now in chaos
We're under the control of hyenas
Yes, hyenas now own us
They've us to gnash
We're finished!

Wake up all sheep
Wake up you sheep
Detach hyenas' grip
Put your fear apart
Just stand intact

Stand up and fight
Fight hyenas
Fight such anathemas

Wherever I go
I see sufferings
Sufferings, sufferings
Sheep are full packed
The numbers are imaginable
I see pregnant sheep
Old and young sheep
I see disabled ones
They're puking on each other
Their faces are contorted
I see no hyenas
I don't seem them in these sufferings
They aren't facing such sufferings
How if they're the ones enacting them
If fear nauseated
The problem is the same

The question is the same
Why hyenas took our barn
Did our ancestors live here really?
Did my mom live here?
Did my dad live here?
Did your parents live here?
I don't believe
I can't believe
How can I suffer this way?
If this were home anyway
Home in this very barn
Hyenas would've been in the den

The barn is for sheep
The den is for hyenas
Neither is it for dogs

Everybody should go home
Home to where he or she belongs
We're tired of hyenas and dogs
We're tired of their abuses
To us they are but curses
There is no excuse
Whenever I say this
This is what it is
We don't need hyenas
Go hyenas go
Go to your no-go

Suffering in the barn like this
How will it be in the den?
Turning the barn into a den
Does it make it a den?
A barn is a barn
And a den is a den
The barn won't permanently be a den
Let the den be a den
And the barn be the barn

When hyenas own a barn
Sheep are in a big pain
They destroy everything
Everything becomes a pain
Whatever sheep think is fine isn't
Hyenas always seek conviviality
That's based on plot
They talk about commonality
Yet, they treat us differently
Hyenas are always guilty
They think sheep suffer from gullibility
When they butcher them with insensitivity
As they swell with pomposity
They keep on believing in irrevocability
Again, isn't this insanity?

We need to change this state
Yes, we must change this state
The state on absurdity
Whereby hyenas demand civility
Which hyenas take for granted

Sheep are not stupid
However they might look timid
Sheep sometimes may be infuriated
They'd end up causing a calamity
They know all of their harassers
They evidence their extravaganza bonanza
Their predators must wait for sheep's shimewaza
That'll fell hyenas like influenza
Hyenas must hear this stanza
Again, it is not about shosholoza
If anything this is lollapalooza

We sheep are tired of their oppression
Surely, we are tired of their destruction
Change is on the horizon
When all hyenas will go back to the den
The time sheep will truly own their barn
This change is inexorable
Getting rid of hyenas is possible
Change is nonnegotiable
We must expel hyenas
Gentlemen and Duenas
All sheep should take on hyenas
No hyena should be spared
We're tired and tired
Let us make the statement

Hyenas have always been irresponsible
Our situation is horrible
Sheep are now knowledgeable
They're determined and able

Sheep will take on hyenas
This is a fact but not propagandas
Sheep get rid of hyenas
Don't fear their teeth and brouhahas
They're like empty containers
Hyenas are nothing but cons

Docile as we may seem
Still we can fathom
We know their harm on us
Hyenas are but a doom to us
We're tired of their greed and unwisdom
Our barn is not their kingdom
We can't always be harum-scrum
We have to solve this conundrum
As we offer this antebellum
Our hearts have been hardened like tantalum

Let me tell the hyenas
Hey hyenas!
Listen and take this for sure
It is the last counsel
Wherever you're
Sheep are now aware
They're ready to dare
Your magic is over
Time to go is here and now
Go back to your netherworld

Go live with the deceased hyenas
Go share your adventures
Share your disasters
Go enjoy your plunders
Go to your masters
The ones who enable you to devour us
The one who'll rob you what you robbed us
Yes go, go and face the consequences

Go hyenas go
Go
Go in your no-go
Go, go

Figure 5 Hyenas in front of their den

The politics of *hyenas*

We see them monkeying around
With their monkey business and pride
Sheep are indeed tired
Tired of hyena's political hanky-panky
They won't listen to any flack
They need their true liberty
Yes, sheep need liberty from hyenas

However we're sheep
We still have brains
Our self-awareness is still with us
However you're hyenas
You still are culpable
All hyenas will end up in a crucible
Never shall they get away with murder

Hey hyenas!
It is time for you to suffer
Take this seriously
Don't think we'll always banter
We're fed up with your canker
Nothing you can now tinker
You better pack up and vanish
May you perish!

For a ride you took us
You played all sorts of stupid games on us
You've always divided us
Divide and rule has always your ruse to use
Hyenas, it is time to get your rewards
Never complain or accuse
You get what you deserve
Go back to the den

That's where you belong
It won't take long
You'll soon see our rage
We want you in the prison
Yes, there's where you deserve to be
I'm talking to all hyenas
The old ones and the wannabe
Hyenas are hyenas
Pack and vanish
May you perish!

Things have changed
All hyenas must be purged
Like plague they must be clashed
All the high and the mighty hyenas
Must be made to go
This does need any argy-bargy
This barn is ours
Their den is theirs
Everybody must belong where he or she belongs
Hyenas can't become hogs
Dolphins can't become dugongs
Dogs are always dogs
Dogs have no credos
Whatever they do is hangdog
Just like hyenas
Whatever they do is selfish
Their goals are always fiendish
We abhor the roles they play to their masters
Yes, hyenas
Rabid dogs
Be they revered for their powers
Hyenas are hyenas

I'm telling all moles among sheep
Those of ours who turned themselves into hyenas
Those whose hiatus has ruined us

We're telling all those greed morons
This message is for all mongrels
Yes, those mules among us
Have always to vend us
They're nothing but wily hyenas
They made us to believe we're all sheep
They put us on a sleep
They used their sweet words
They made everything creepy
What we know is demise
We know nothing but miseries
They've always fed on us
They've always feasted on us
Sheep must make this their onus
To purge all hyenas
Never look into their faces
Hyenas must go

Tell all those suffering from proclivity for authority
Their greed turned them into hyenas
All those embracing absurdity for authority
Their rust makes them mere hyenas
Tell them to stop their imbecility
They'll be treated like hyenas
They slaughter and laugh at their preys
Such are hyena's manners
Beasts with such tendencies are but hyenas
Humans with such comportment are but hyenas
Hyenas are hyenas
Be they human hyenas or whatever genre of hyenas
Political hyenas
Economical hyenas
Ethical hyenas
Hyenas are hyenas
Never trust hyenas
Never spare hyenas

Sheep are utterly tired
They're indeed tired
Tired of being pigged on
Tired of sheer obliteration
They're tired of exploitation
Sheep are tired of violation
Yes, sheep are tired
They need to be emancipated
They need to be understood
For this statement clearly made
Hyenas have to pack and go
Yes they'd quickly go

This is the land of the sheep
So, it must, indeed, belong to sheep
Whoever that doesn't look like sheep
Should not rule the sheep
Hyenas go rule hyenas
This isn't the land of hyenas
Sheep will no longer endorse hyenas
They're tired of their hoo-has
They won't buy ballyhoos
This can't go on by all means
Hyenas should pack and vanish
Sheep should take their dominion
Yes, sheep must own and control the barn
All oppressed creatures must control their destiny
All exploited should control their production
This is a revolution
Yes, call it sheep revolution

We're tired of corrupted minds
We're fed up with polluted minds
We are pissed off with rash minds
We're tired of violated minds
We want to reinvent ourselves
We're on the way to liberate ourselves

We know the onus is on us
We're sheep by nurture
We aren't sheep by nature
We're tired of this culture
The culture of the vultures
The culture of making others pastures
We're Homo sapiens

I know there are many sheep
I see them everywhere
Some might not be aware
That sheep they are
Yet the same are sheep
They may live under normal fear
Fear of not accepting to fight for the sheep
All sheep everywhere
Need to take on hyenas
Be they rabid dogs or real hyenas
Sheep real and manmade must take on hyenas

Who denies that he or she isn't a sheep?
If you aren't sheep
Then you're hyena
I see two groups of protagonists
Sheep and hyenas
I see only two antagonists
Irreconcilable opponents
If you're not with us
Then you are against us
You need to declare your allegiance
We don't co-opt hermaphrodites
If you're a true sheep declare it
For those who hastate
We know they're but hyenas
Hyenas must go away
Away to the den
Where they must be confined

Waiting to get their rewards
Where they used to confine the sheep

I am furious and flabbergasted
Every sheep is anxiously prepared
Sheep are determined
They seriously want to usher in their liberation
They want to see all sheep liberated
They're no long inebriated by tricks and lies
Yes, the denigrations hyenas have always offered
They're aware of all plots
To have them scampered
This time it won't work
Why should it work?
While sheep know all ruses
Honorable hyenas should go
Let them go to the gaols
Let them head for the gallows
Where they used to confine sheep

Sheep are innocent
Hyenas have full of culpability
Everybody knows this reality
This is why all sheep need to fight
All sheep must stand
Sheepishness must come to an end
We must decide
We're all creatures
Nobody should exploit another
Nobody should fear another
Let us take on this chasm
Let's restore justice
Let's face this verity

Some sheep cooperate with hyenas
They betray their brethren
Some hyenas pretend to be sheep

91

They pretend to care about sheep
Indeed, all betrayers are offenders
They are all pretenders
All of those are betrayers
Sheep will never be hyenas
And hyenas will never be sheep
I have said this time after time
Even if they change their names
Hyenas are hyenas
Even if sheep carry hyena's names
They will never become hyenas
Even if hyenas carry sheep's names
Surely, they will never become sheep
The chasm between the duos is deep
Deep and deep
Nobody can close this gap
This gap will always be there
It has always been there
Let's face this verity

Hyenas have dug in their heels
They've committed all evils
They've created classes
Sheep are sheep
What are classes for?
Whatever class they are put in
It won't change anything
Sheep are sheep
Nobody can have it to grasp
Hyenas becoming sheep!
I feel like making a yelp!
Sheep must remain sheep
Innocent as they've always been
This what we're
We're sheep
This is who we are
We are innocent

Guilty are the hyenas
This what they're
They wrongly called us sheep
They thereafter devoured us
Let us assume their ruse
Let us use it to show them their farce

Hyena in sheep's clothing

THE MORAL HYPOCRISY OF THE BIBLE BELT

Figure 6 the hyena in sheep's clothing

Can you detect hyenas in sheep's clothing?
Some may say yes you can
Others may say you cannot
Whatever it is
It was not easy for us
To know we'd end up in this mess
Do you know what brought us to this mess?
We wanted to live just like others
Our clothing on hyenas deceived us
We trusted hyenas in sheep's clothing
We suspected nothing
We wrongly thought hyenas were sheep
Not just because we're insane
Also, it isn't because we're blind
We wrongly thought they're sheep
We thought they're like us

Again, are we alone in this deceit?
How many have suffered the same fate

I see them all over the place
Yet I can't condemn them like others do to us
Nobody wants to end up in this mess
Importantly, one's to stand up and fight
Yes, sheep have to fight
Fiercely we've to fight

Nobody will ever trust hyenas
Enceinte with greed
Even fools can't trust hyenas
This is why we need them to go
We need all to agree indeed
Sheep must make hyenas go
Go hyenas go
Go hyenas go

I call upon hyenas to pack and vanish
Please don't ignore to dispatch
Don't treat me like journalists
Whom some call unprivileged belligerents
Take this communication seriously
Sheep are changing dramatically
Whatever they do now they do it meticulously
They're fed up with hyenas' perfidy
What stinking perfidy!
We thought we're all beasts
We thought we'd protect each other
Aren't we all devoured by the lions?
Aren't we preyed on by vampires?
Aren't we devoured by monsters?

Sheep are determined to fight
This is the only fact
We'll try even if we die
Even if stakes are high
If need be we better die
Why'd we live why?

95

While we're eaten like a pie
Is there anybody that'll never die?
By accentuating this fact
Sheep are determined to fight
For, death is a fact
Nobody will avert it
Why should we worry?
While we know it will one day come?
Why cowering
As if we will live forever

We'll never stop fighting
We'll never stop contemplating
Sheep have to fight
Truly all sheep have to fight
All types of sheep have to fight day and night
Better die fighting
Rather than live nerve-wracking

Who wants to wait for death?
The best way is to confront *death*
In this gamble you may win
Better lose expecting to win
Why fear while you live under the Sun
Why cower whereas you don't know when
Is there anybody who knows the day of his or her death?
This is the fact
Work on this element
Fear is but illusion
All sheep need to fear misapprehension
Stand and fight on
Fear nothing but fear

Although hyenas kill us
Will they live forever?
Aren't they afraid of us?
Yet they kill us

Why do we cower?
While we know nobody's forever
Does this need a philosopher to uncover?
Sheep wake up and fight
Fight for your fate

Seeing hyenas living high life
Seeing hyenas enjoying life
All is at our expenses
All is at our loses
Why don't we take on them?
For how long are we to fear them
Does our fear improve our lives?
We better fight for our lives
We better die fighting
Rather than live waiting for pangs
Who wants political gangbangs?
Aren't hyenas like boomslangs?
Their poison of division is like birth pangs
Do birth pangs stop mothers from bringing more sugars?
Where would the world have been?
Had all mothers cowered before birth pangs

Let us pit ourselves against hyenas
Let's push the envelope
For this is only our hope
We need to change the landscape
No hyena will get a chance to escape
We'll choke them with a towrope
However it might sound like a guttersnipe
The message is clear
Whoever that wants to hear must hear
Sheep are ready to take on hyenas

Those with wisdom should hear
Sheep want to make this clear

This time we're unstoppable
Our force is as fierce as a volcano
We'll not spare any wino
Sheep will charge like an angry rhino
The barn will be on the inferno
Take this news is pro bono
Never underestimate it like a soprano
Good news always is
We've nothing to lose

If you're not a grass eater
Whoever you're
To us, you're with the hyenas
We'll treat you like hyenas
If you don't live like us
You're not one of us
To us, you're but a hyena
Every sheep will take on every hyena

This is our time of awakening
We're tired of all this skiving
We've suffered for long
This is time for us to make a declaration
The declaration of emancipation
Yes, we need emancipation
True and real emancipation
The time we've been under hyenas is enough
We need to prove that we're tough
This message should be taken seriously
I warn those thinking it isn't a hiccough
Please take this message seriously
Sheep are now awake

This time the *barn* will explode
Every sheep will take a panade
This doesn't need any serenade
Our enemies we'll assault

They must expect bastinadoes
We'll explode like volcanoes
In defiance of the subterfuges
For long we've been divided
This time we're united
For a long time we've cowered
This time we'll stand
Hyenas should be taught a lesson
The lesson that they've never given a damn

Like ants we'll stand together
Like puffer fish we'll become even tougher
Our aim is to assail our slaughterer
We'll punish this adder
This time we'll turn table on him or her
We are tired of exploitation
We're fed up with humiliation
For how long will we bear indignation?
This is but a time for the explosion
The explosion whose repercussions will affect every hyena
This is the time for all sheep to stand together
Come all sheep wherever you're
This time if for your emancipation

Whoever eats us is a hyena
For, does exactly what other hyenas do
Sheep have suffered horribly
None has suffered far more than us
It is time for emancipating ourselves
All sheep need to strand together and fight
This song is the only message
Gather courage
Take it and work on it
Hyenas must go to the den
Whether they like it or not
Theirs is a den
Ours is a barn

The politics of sheep

Sheep need organization
They must avoid deception
Theirs must be clean politics
The politics of equality
The politics of justice
The politics of peace

Sheep are naturally peaceful
Yet, they can be vengeful
Once they're duped and molested
For long sheep have been provoked
Nobody should go on with this
My friends take no chance
Sheep are not as stupid as hyenas
They're courageous and wise
Once they decide to say enough is enough
Everything can become a bit rough

Sheep need their barn
They're not ready to live in the den
Sheep won't go on with this
They now need true modification
They need their lives back
They need their barn back
Please hyenas go home
Home to the den you belong
Go to the den you're used to

The politics of sheep is about justice
They don't want any interference
They abhor violence
However this should not be taken as weakness
Shall our adversaries embark on violence

Nobody will ever budge
Theirs is but justice
Yes, justice
Sheep need justice
They're not begging for justice
Please take this earnestly
Sheep are now courageous
They'll take on whoever it is
The one who wants to take them for a ride
Whoever that's them deceived
He'd get prepared
Things have changed
Sheep need liberation

Sheep are fed up with the politics of being eaten
They openly declare their new vision
The vision of true emancipation
Long gone is the politics of suffocation
We want true democracy
We want tangible existence
We openly declare
Being eaten no more

We want to take control of our destiny
This is our new epiphany
We've suffered enough agony
Let all know now
Let all hear it now
We're not joking
We're not even trying
We know what we want
We know how to get
We'll take on hyenas
Hyenas must go to the den

We're tired of hypocrisy
Saying we're all equal

Hyenas and sheep can't be equal
They have always been different
They will always be different
This difference is permanent
This we need to accept
This doesn't need any tutor
Sheep know who they're
Everybody know who they're

Hyenas slurping our sweat
On top of eating our meat
My foot!
This is their end
The end of the end
Or call it the beginning of the end
The end of being maltreated
The end of our oppressors is approaching
I can see it on the horizon
Oppressors will never win
If they do is for a short time
The end of our killers is closing in
Things can't go on this way
Although our killers are carried away
Thinking they're nifty
Soon they'll get the message

Hyenas will get their message
Yes, the message of their demise
There won't be anything to assuage
The oppressed must gather courage
They must be as tough like robber crabs
They must harden their skulls and ribs
For this is their opportune time
Never waste any time
Take on the hyenas
Kick them out of all barns
Let them go to where they belong

Sheep be strong
Your liberation is on the egress
So, never digress
Never stop this course
The course of emancipation

Never allow hyenas to stymie you
As they pit one against another
Never fall asunder
Just stand together
I truly tell you
You'll get your rights
Go fight for your rights
Nobody can give you these rights
You're the ones to grab them
Take them
They're yours
Agitate for them
Make 'em permanently yours

I know how bestially you're treated
I know how your ways were despised
Yet you heroically prevailed
You lived through all sorts of torments
It is your time to speak aloud
Yes, it is time to fight for rights
It is time to air your thoughts
The time is now

Kings of *hyenas*

Figure 7 Hyena kings

I see insane kings of hyenas
They're young and old
Everything they do is odd
They're but cowards
They don't want to think about their ends
They've committed atrocities of all kinds
They pretend to be modest
Horrible!
Never gamble
They're not humble
They're but ogres

A hyena is hyena
I've said this earlier
Be it a servant or a master
The hyena will act as a hyena
This beast is immoral

Greed is its vector

Being kings or empresses
Hyenas won't become seraphs
They'll always be led by their bellies
They're greedy and ferocious
This will never change
Theirs is to cause damage

What they say isn't what they do
They're as greedy as a komodo
Never entrust your life to komodo
Whatever they say is but innuendos
They depend on their aficionados
Yet they preach democracy!

These kings of hyenas are evil
Most of them don't want to go
They always live in a no-go
They're the prisoners of their egos
They depend on their commandos
To make sure they'd not go
They hate every aficionado
That tells them to go
They live like mungos mungo
They'd like you to make do
When they live in paradise

Hyena kings are as corrupt as Lucifer
Never think kings of hyenas are sober
Everybody is nothing but a profiteer
Let me make this clear
Never err, my dear
Hyena kings are but sinister

Lying is their weapon
Threatening is their truncheon

They care not about humans
They care about their ambitions
Their brains are in their tummies
Their heads are but dummies
Time to stop such ambitions is now
Nobody should allow this mess to grow

Beware of hyena kings
They've caused a lot of sufferings
Theirs is always trappings
Even if it means to kill all ewes
To them ewes are but nothing
Their rights have no meaning

Hyena kings are but heartless creatures
Compare them with vultures
Thuggery is one of their cultures
To them all of us are but stooges
They're happy to see us suffering
Given that they always will be enjoying

I call upon all the oppressed
Stand united and determined
Our barn needs to be cleared
All hyenas must hit the road
Barn is for sheep
And den is for hyenas
Sing this psalm of yours
Sing and recite it in your homes
This psalm is yours
Take it and preserve

Hyena kings like the *status quo*
Disobedience needs to be our *quid pro quo*
We don't need any dialogue
Why if at all we're facing fatigue
For whatever they've done to us

We need to embark on disobedience
I call on civil disobedience
Fear not their violence
Fear not their police
Nobody can stop the mass
Once it decides, say enough is enough
So, just tough it out
Show them the way
Never cow before their trickery

Kings don't care about others
What they care about is their powers
Many have caused disasters
To see to it they remain in office
Yet this power is not theirs
The power they call theirs is ours
They have tampered with constitutions
They have corrupted institutions
Parliaments have become rubber stamps
To bless their delinquency
We need to stand and say nope

They've set bad precedents
They've became political accidents
They've hardened their hearts
To see to it they don't face reality
My goodness!
This time they'll go
No mercy,
They'd be made to go
Hell no!
They must go

They're sitting on heaps of a mess
Ruling forever is theirs
Yet they fail to recognize
That one time they'll go

107

I'm sure they'll go
It is time for them to go
Yes, the mass must say go
When the mass say "go"
They may ignore any jingo
Their power they'll forgo
This must come to fruition
Yes, the fruition is liberation

They've committed sacrileges
Through their acts and verbiages
They've robbed people of all ages
Justice has suffered miscarriages
We need to resuscitate justice
No meaningful life without justice

They've superimposed themselves on us
While they're ridiculously careless about us
With pomp and ruckus
They dupe us
Saying they love us
While they truly hate us

They've ruined our lives
Nothing is left of us
We're but their prisoners
Again, they are but dying asses
For, we won't give in
We will keep on soldiering on
We have to kick ass
Let tell the mass
They need to stand
And fight for their rights

We don't need to be afraid of them
Let's cause them mayhem
They must get out of the helm

We must disobey kingdom
Usually, kings are afraid of us
They know the power our unity gives us

The kingdom of hyenas is meaningless
Kings rule with heartlessness
They've created a mess
Let's remove this morass
With our hands we must remove the untidiness
With our voice we must fight against this chaos
We need to be callous
Never look into their faces
Like monkey, we must put them behind bars

Most hyenas' kings are maniacs
This is the hallmark of all megalomaniacs
They eat us like freaks
They wrongly think we're lunatics

They've forgotten we're patriots
We'll destroy them with their sycophants
We've no more semantics
But to take on these power fanatics

They've turned our countries into private estates
What an understatement!
Now that we're vehement
This is our assignment

Kamikaze as we are
Now that we're aware
We'll never worry to dare
Our house to launder
This is our sacred obligation
We need to bring liberation

They've their tentacles everywhere
Let them hear this canticle everywhere
Nobody we'll spare
We're going nowhere
Ours is to cut their appendages
They should get prepared for manacles

We'll stand our ground
We'll hunt them like hounds
Their heads we'll pound
They'll walk with fire tires around

We're no ostriches anymore
We won't hide our heads under wings
Never shall we bury our head in sands
Upon seeing our nemeses
We'll take them without any mercy

Before their citizens hyena kings are like angels
Behind the curtains,
They are but devils
They commit all known and unknown evils
They turn their people into fools
Again, their people know everything
Yet, they pretend to know nothing

Though they fool their peoples
They too are fooled by mongrels
They are surrounded by falsifiers
Those enabling them to cause miseries
They don't read the signs of time
They end up in bedlam

They're fooled by their courtiers
Those who devour their leftovers
They all live in palavers
Indeed, they're all deceivers

110

Though they all know it
They try to avoid it

They live like gods
Some die like dogs
When hit with tongs
Till they puke their tongues
They die in agonies
Shame becomes their fortune

They are surrounded by pretenders
They make them feel great
Yet all is but mere deceit
They don't get that
Like bees theirs is fire
Their lives are but a satire

Hyena kings live in their cocoons
Ensconced amidst goons
They're surrounded by buffoons
Singing their phony admirations
When the drama comes to expiration
Everybody run to his bend

They are like wild dogs
They are hunted like hogs
They can't laugh even at dogs
They're always in ping-pongs
For, they're but nothing
And their power is nothing

Like a mourning gecko on the rock
Hyena kings own no flock
Whatever they do is but a fluke
Power belong to the flock
Yet they pretend to own it
And they assume they are everything

Birds laugh at them
Mountains and valleys curse them
They know their harm
Their legacies are sham
If anything, it is but chicanery
And what they do is but trickery

Hyena kings fear their own shadows
They are always in the middle
Their brains are shallow
Their views are narrow
They end up perishing
For something they saw coming

We saw it in some quarters
Hyena kings had their quivers
The day they met with their killers
Some ended in the gallows
Lucky ones died in exile
All become futile

Greedy queens of hyenas

Hyena kings are not alone
They eat along with their queens
They eat flesh and bones
They feed on every person
Call them whatever
In reality they're not queens
They're freaks and flukes
For, some act like goons

They're as extravagant as nabobs
They pay no hoot
When they enjoy their loots
They careless about subjects
Theirs has always been pilfering us
They are but vampires
They have turns us into their empires
Their hearts are rusted
They need not to be trusted

They spend as if there's no tomorrow
What we know from them is but sorrow
They've sucked our marrow
We're trying as a helpless a sparrow
When her chicks face a viper
The difference is she is innocent however

They lost sense of motherhood
The time their husbands stood
They declared their kinghood
Their wives too declared their queen hood
Their queens then conspired
To rule behind the curtains
Where they act like ruffians

113

They pretend to speak for mothers
Yet, what they do is but disasters
They're only mother users
Thugs, criminals and robbers
This what they're
Though outward they glare

They eat with legs and hands
This is the tendency of all brigands
Given that we're gallants
We need to fell these hooligans
I assure you we'll win
This is the time to win

We're tired of these Ettarres
They contaminate our altars
Why eating like jackals
Why keeping these criminals
Why keeping them while we're starving
Why'd tolerate them while we're suffering

Some of them are as fat as grub worms
They're in all shapes and all forms
We'll become their phantoms
We're tired of their norms
We need to uphold our laws
Nobody should be above our laws

Figure 8 Grub worm

We now need change
We'll take no chance
There won't be any exchange
When time for change arises
There won't be any bribes and patronage
Never make do with vagabondage

Our bodies are tired
Our hearts are shattered
Our souls are wounded
This must come to an end
Again who'll do it?
Indeed, this is our duty

We've consciousness
Just like any human beings
We're pushed by this consciousness
To take on our oppressors
This has no negotiation

Till we get real and true liberation

It is through this consciousness
We're inviting the mass
Please come *en masse*
Come for the noble cause
You've nothing to lose
It is only the chains that you'll miss

Come and never be afraid
Never live your weapon behind
Bear in mind
Never fear to end up in quod
Better dying on your feet
Than living on your knees

Hyena queens are de facto rulers
They corner their partners
They cause many dangers
When they usurp powers
They pretend not to know this veracity
At their hearts
They're eaten by this fright

Sheep know them all
And above all,
They know how they fall
Save they're afraid
For how long will they be afraid?
Will fear bring them bread?

Queens rule from behind the curtains
Their powers are like mountains
They words are cannons
Unchecked are their influences
Who can touch on the untouchable?
Again, is this desirable?

They rob the kingdoms
Just from the bedrooms
You don't see them in any boardrooms
Yet, their businesses enjoy a boom
They lobby in the banks
They get their checks

Some are illiterates
Yet, they live like literati
Power is in their hands intact
They've nothing to doubt about
Whom should they fear?
The army is under their power
Everything is under their muscle
Kings are under their control

Queens especially use many wiles
They mostly depend on lies
They pretend they love lambs
While they hate them behind curtains
On faces it is all sneers
At hearts, it is disgust and laughter

Many portend to be anthropologists
At hearts they are but shoplifts
They use their notorieties
To make many profits
How can they love people while they rob them?
Nobody matters to them except their piggishness

Some form phony companies
They give them good names
They pretend they're for good causes
Behind the curtain they steal monies
Those charities are but pipes
That they use to rob the innocent earthlings

117

Figure 9 Queen Hyena

The prince and princesses

On top of keeping kings and queens
Sheep keep princes and princesses
They act like their parents
They do the same monkey businesses
They enjoy themselves while the people suffer
They're but wolves that care not about our grief

They rob the mass
Ill-gotten wealth they amass
Like their parents, they're above laws
Like parasites are on our backs
Parents' power gives them prowess
To plunder as they please
Who can prevent them while power is theirs?
To who are they responsible while they've no voters

Some are groomed by their parents
To take power when they vacate
Sheep just watch
Now they've to stop it
Some have already taken on it
The rest need to follow suit

Once their parents get powers
They automatically become rulers
They enjoy power accessories
Business becomes their endeavors
Just like any robbers they terrorize our den
They eat us and our children

The end

This is the end
Not the end of the world
It is the end of the melody
Importantly it must be said
Take your verses
Read them aloud
They are your verses

Go proclaim emancipation
All sheep must stand up
In all nations they're in
Sheep should speak up
They must tell everyone
This is the time
Time for liberation
This is the time
It is the time of time
Time for fruition

I pray for thee
So that you can lead to an apogee
Yes, without any melee
All of you who are suffering
Put this in the mind
These verses set your bearing
Just be strong
Never waive

I wish you all well
Go everybody tell
Tell them about the verses
Read the verses

I call upon all *sheep*
Never be on the hop
Fighting is the only hope
Pay no beep
Take on hyenas
Stop your sufferings

Reclaim your barns
Send hyenas to their dens
All of you've my prayers
Stop all palavers
Stand for peace
Stand for justice
Stand for emancipation

Let me doff here
Blessed be all
I love you all
I pray for you all
I pray your true God
I pray Mulungu the only God
Who created you the way you're
Importantly, of all
Restore
Rejuvenate
Reclaim
Proclaim
The nobility of your ways
Abandon colonial ways
Go back to your ways
It is only through your ways
You can progress
Enough is enough
Repeat together
Say
Enough is enough

I pray for thee all
Blessed be all
All that'll read this tome
I authoritatively hand down the psalm
The psalm of the oppressed
Come all oppressed
Take your psalm
Go sing it
Go preach it
Go guard it
Go treasure it
It is the only one you have

Figure 10 the state house

Printed in the United States
By Bookmasters